IF YOU WERE A...

Teacher

IF YOU WERE A...
Teacher

Virginia Schomp

BENCHMARK BOOKS

MARSHALL CAVENDISH
NEW YORK

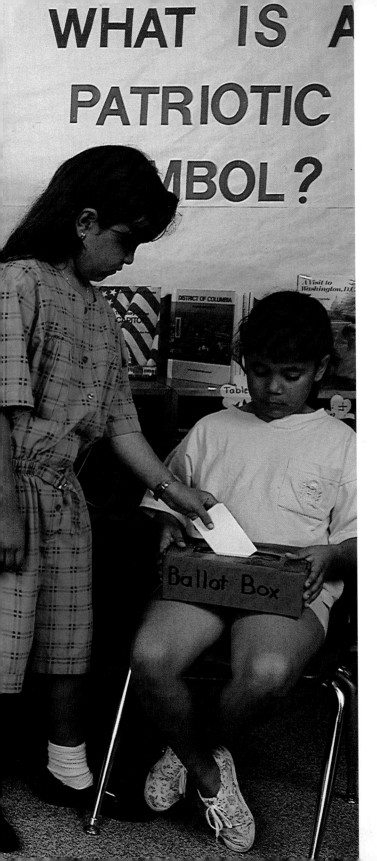

Voting in a class election helps students learn how to be good citizens.

If you were a teacher, you would share a great gift—learning. You would help children learn how to live and work in the world.

Today your students are voting. As they choose a class president, they are learning about elections and government. Tomorrow you might help them find out how fish swim. Next week they'll discover dinosaurs on a trip to the museum.

Each day is different in the classroom. And all your days would be filled with new ideas and discoveries if you were a teacher.

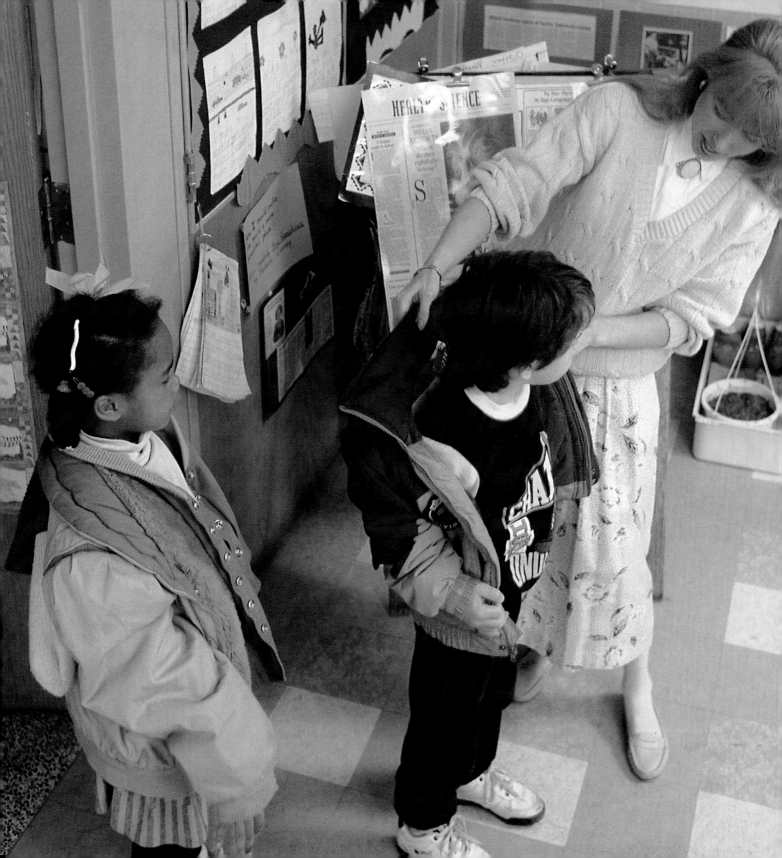

Drawings and decorations make the classroom a fun place to work and play.

The bell rings. Children chatter. It's the first day of school. Today teachers and students start a new adventure together.

This teacher works in an elementary school. Elementary schools usually include kindergarten and grades one through six or one through eight. In most elementary schools, teachers stay with the same class of children all year. They get to know all about each member of their classroom "family."

A friendly hello helps children feel at home on the first day of school.

Subjects taught in elementary school include reading, writing, and math. Teachers also may give lessons in science, social studies, health, and computers.

A reading lesson is one of the most important parts of the schoolteacher's day.

Most important of all, teachers want students to have fun while they learn. A teacher knows that children who love to learn have the best chance of doing well all through life.

The school day includes time for practicing penmanship and learning about the world through science experiments.

Textbooks, worksheets, charts, maps—teachers use all kinds of printed materials to make lessons clear. Good teachers also use unusual materials and activities to share the excitement of learning.

If you were a teacher, you might bring a story to life with hand puppets.

This teacher's pint-size partner makes storytime extra fun.

A feathered visitor gives students a close-up look at wildlife.

To make math fun, you could play a lively card game. Your lesson on wild animals really takes off when you invite a barn owl to class!

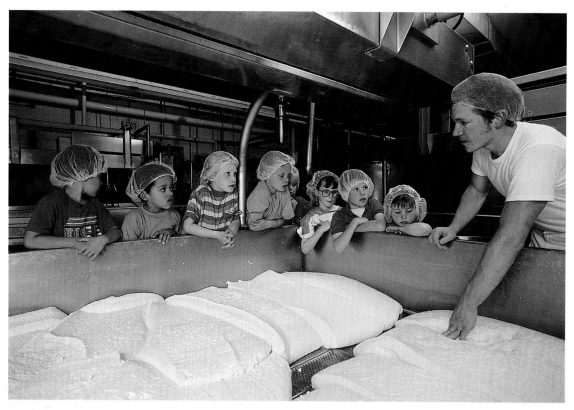

A cheese factory tour spices up a lesson on food production.

Sometimes the best way to teach is to get out of the classroom. Field trips to museums, factories, and other interesting places give children a better understanding of a subject than any textbook can.

Are your students learning about nature? A trip through a wildlife preserve gives them a close-up look. Studying reptiles? In a book, a hissing snake is just another picture. In the hands, it's downright impressive!

For these girls, meeting a hissing king snake is the most exciting part of their field trip to a science museum.

Art class helps this girl create a beautiful world with paper and paint.

Most elementary school teachers give lessons in many subjects to one class. But some teach one "special subject" to all the children in the school.

Art and music are special subjects. In many elementary schools, art teachers go from class to class, teaching students different ways to paint and draw. Music teachers help singers blend their voices in song. They teach young musicians how to turn squeaks and scratches into silvery notes.

In many elementary schools, the first instrument students learn to play is the recorder.

14

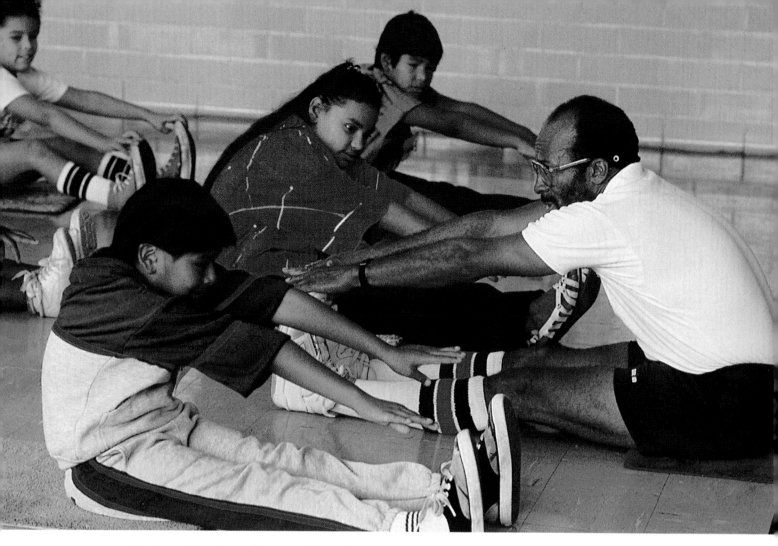

A phys ed teacher shows students how to warm up their muscles before playing sports.

Physical education is another special subject. For many schoolchildren, gym class is the best part of the day. That's because, in gym, they get a chance to be active . . . and loud!

Sit-ups, push-ups, jumping jacks—exercise makes children healthy and strong. Gymnastics builds strength and body control. Students have fun learning the basic skills of sports like track, soccer, and basketball. Could one of these young athletes be a future sports superstar?

Playing on the school soccer team gives children a chance to exercise and have fun.

Special education teachers help children who have special needs. This girl cannot hear. The teacher helps her practice reading lips and pronouncing sounds.

Some children have trouble learning to read. If you were a special education teacher, you would use tests to find out what's causing the problem. You would work with the class-room teacher to plan ways to overcome it. How proud you feel the first time your student reads a storybook out loud!

Feeling the way her teacher's throat vibrates helps this girl learn how to pronounce different sounds.

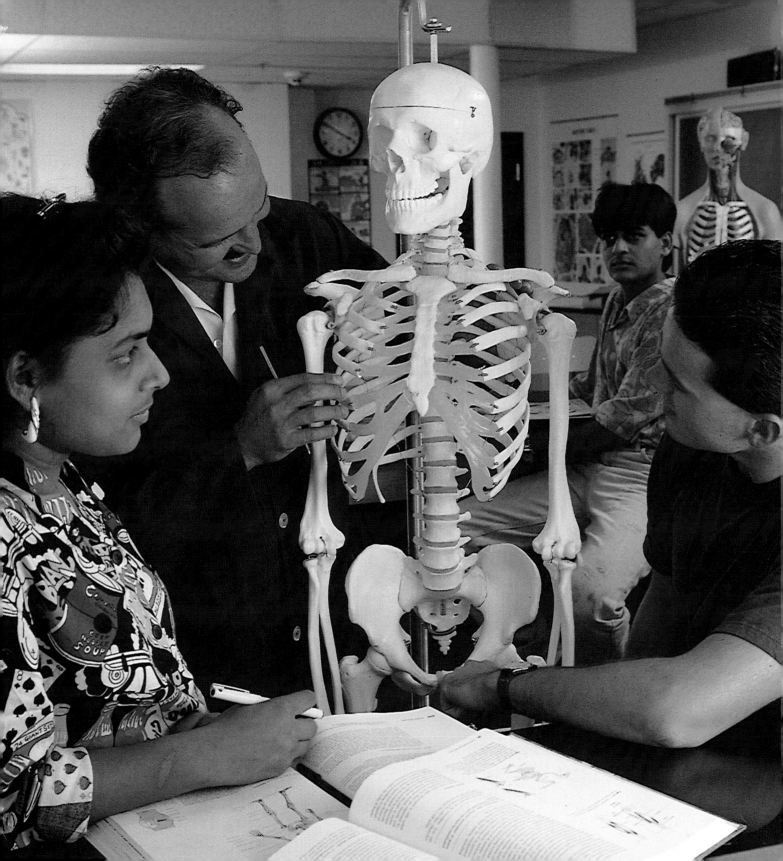

Job training may include a class in auto mechanics.

After elementary school, students go on to middle school, then high school. Teachers in these schools are experts in one subject. Some teach science, math, social studies, art, music, or physical education. Others give lessons in English, foreign languages, or job training.

The school day in middle and high schools is divided into periods. Each period, students go to a different classroom. Teachers may give the same lesson to a different group of students five times in one day. The students all have different needs and interests, and that makes each class a new adventure.

A bony buddy helps a high school science teacher explain the human body.

Teachers spend many after-school hours reviewing and planning lessons.

The final bell rings. Students fly out the doors. But for teachers, the school day is not over yet.

Some teachers grade papers and plan lessons after school.

Others help with activities such as the chess club and the student newspaper. In the gym, the phys ed teacher is coaching the basketball team. In the auditorium, art and music teachers help students get ready for a school play.

A high school basketball coach helps her team plan some winning moves.

School's out!

Summer at last! Both teachers and students enjoy taking a break from schoolwork during summer vacations. It's fun to relax with family and friends. Summer also gives teachers time to take classes that help them keep up-to-date with school subjects.

Many teachers have summer jobs. Some tutor students who need extra help with math or reading. Others may work as camp counselors or even firefighters.

All teachers remember the special times they spent with their students and wonder what adventures the new school year will bring.

Working with younger children helps these students find out if they have what it takes to become a good teacher.

Do you enjoy learning? Do you like helping others to learn? Are you hardworking and patient? These are some of the qualities you will need if you want to become a teacher.

To earn a teaching license, you must go to college. There you will study the subjects you want to teach. You will learn the best ways to share new ideas with students.

Teaching is hard work. It is also fun and exciting to change students' lives with the gift of learning.

A teacher's most important tools include imagination, patience, and understanding.

TEACHERS IN TIME

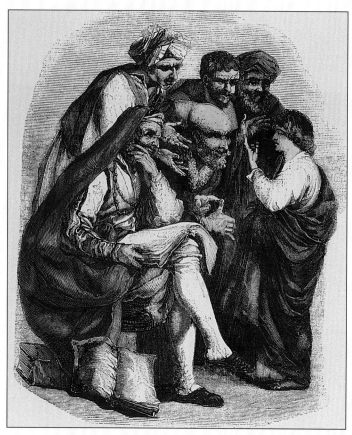

A group of educated Hebrew men teach a boy about religious laws. The ancient Hebrews were one of the first peoples who believed in educating both the rich and the poor.

In ancient Greece, students learned reading, writing, arithmetic, music, dancing, and gymnastics. Our modern system of education is based on ideas that began with the Greeks.

In the Middle Ages, from about A.D. 500 to 1500, students in Europe were educated by priests or monks at schools run by the Christian church. In this painting, a teacher is reading from a holy book.

In the American colonies, teachers in one-room schoolhouses gave lessons in reading, writing, and religion. The boy standing against the wall is wearing a "dunce cap" as a punishment for slow learning.

A TEACHER'S CLOTHING AND TOOLS

Teachers dress neatly and carefully, for a businesslike appearance.

A teacher's tools include: blackboards; slide projectors; computers; pencils, pens, and paper.

WORDS TO KNOW

citizen A member of a country. Being a citizen gives a person special rights and responsibilities.

election Choosing someone or something by voting.

government The way a country, state, or other place is ruled or managed.

middle school A school that usually includes grades five or six through eight. In some places, it is called junior high school.

reptile A cold-blooded animal that crawls on its belly or creeps on short legs. Snakes, lizards, alligators, and turtles are reptiles.

tutor To give private lessons to a student.

wildlife preserve An area set aside for the protection of wild animals.

This book is for Ronnie Cohen,
teacher at the George L. Cooke School, Monticello, New York,
in appreciation of her amazing gift for giving

Benchmark Books
Marshall Cavendish Corporation
99 White Plains Road
Tarrytown, New York 10591
Copyright© 2000 by Marshall Cavendish Corporation

Library of Congress Cataloging-in-Publication Data
Schomp, Virginia
If you were a—teacher / Virginia Schomp.
p. cm.
Includes index.
SUMMARY: Describes what teachers do on a daily basis and the skills and training necessary to become a good teacher.
ISBN 0-7614-0916-5
1. Teachers—Juvenile literature. 2. Teaching—Vocational guidance—Juvenile literature. [1. Teachers. 2. Teaching—Vocational guidance. 3. Occupations. 4. Vocational guidance.] I. Title.
LB1775 .S3453 1999 371.1'0023—dc21 99-34643 CIP

Photo research by Rose Corbett Gordon.

Front cover:courtesy of *Woodfin Camp*:James Wilson
Index Stock Imagery:Jeff Greenberg,1; Bill Bachmann, 4–5; Frank Siteman, 6,8,14; Robert Finken,13. *Woodfin Camp*:Susan Lapides,2; James Wilson, 30(center right). *The Image Bank*: Mel DiGiacomo,7, 30(top); Don Klumpp,11; Alvis Upitis,12; Lou Jones, 20; Juan Silva, 21; L.D.Gordon,23; Jeff Cadge, 24–25,27; Alan Becker, 31. *National Education Association:*9(left & right),30(bottom). *Allsport:*Simon Bruty,17. *The Image Works:*Ellen Senisi,10; Elizabeth Crews,15; Bob Daemmrich,16;Alan Carey,18–19; John Eastcoff /Yva Momatiuk,26 (bottom); Michael Siluk,30(center left). *Virginia Schomp:*22,26(top). *North Wind Picture Archives:*28(top& bottom),29 (bottom). *Art Resource,NY:*Scala,29(top).

Printed in Hong Kong
1 3 5 7 8 6 4 2

INDEX